Hedge Fund
Trading Strategies
Detailed Explanation Of The
Long/Short Margin Ratio Hedge
130/30 80/20 140/60 25/75 150/50

AN INVESTING NEWSLETTER

HEDGE STRATEGIES ™

…offering impersonal, general and indirect opinion

A Moderate Strategy

ISBN 1453763473
EAN 978-1-453-76347-6

1. Hedge-Fund 2. Hedgefund 3. Derivatives 4. Long-Short 5. Long 6. Short 7. Investing 8. Strategies 9. Trading 10. Hedged-Box 11. Short-Against-The-Box 12. Options 13. Exchange-Traded-Fund 14. ETF 15. 130-30 16. 80-20 17. 140/60 18. 25/75 19. 150/50 20. Margin 21. Ratio

Printed in the United States of America

STRATEGY DESCRIPTION AND EXPANATION
For The
Long/Short Margin Ratio Hedge
Moderate Strategy

The mission of the Hedge Strategies newsletter is to educate the average American to the investing advantages enjoyed by the wealthy. The most important advantage is hedging an investment account against loss from falling markets and security prices.

Average Americans may not have $5 million dollars to invest with a legitimate hedge fund, but they can learn the strategies that hedge funds employ for the investment accounts of wealthy clients and apply that knowledge for their own benefit.

Though no professional hedge fund manager will share exactly how he or she hedges, it can be done in only one of fourteen fundamental ways (from seven investment classes and five markets):

1. Long Equity
2. Short Equity
3. Long Equity Option
4. Short Equity Option
5. Long Equity Index Future
6. Short Equity Index Future
7. Long Currency
8. Short Currency
9. Long Interest Rate
10. Short Interest Rate
11. Long Commodity
12. Short Commodity
13. Long CFD
14. Short CFD

The most common hedge fund strategy is the Long/Short. The Long/Short can be built with shares of primary securities, such as stock and exchange traded fund (ETF) shares. The individual investor intending to use this strategy must trade from a margin available investment account.

Conventional wisdom states that risk is positively correlated to investment position return, where exposure to more risk provides the opportunity for higher return.

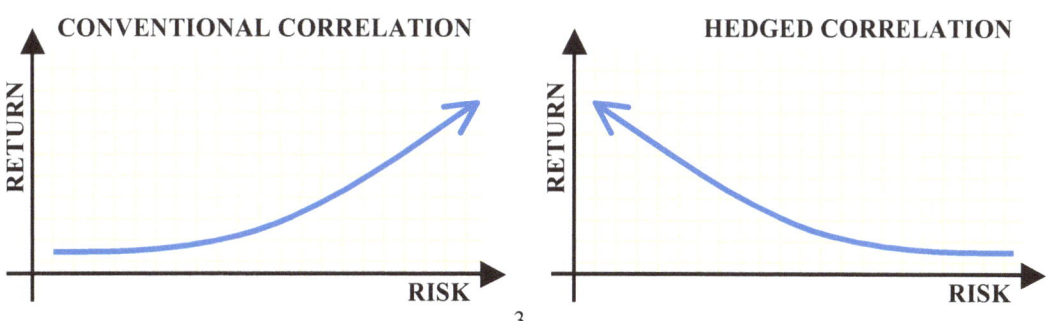

However, when one uses any of the hedging methodologies outlined in Hedge Strategies reports, risk is negatively correlated to investment position return, and creates an environment in which trading strategies with less risk provide the opportunity for higher returns.

A long/short strategy comes in many forms. The more complex strategies use derivatives substituted for primary securities, achieving greater returns through leverage. The long or short components can be traded in different markets. But, in its simplest iteration, using primary securities, each strategy form can be identified as a ratio, such as the 130/30, the 150/50 or the 25/75. These ratios identify the weighting of the investment position components to be held, either long as an investment or short as a position.

The *net investment position* identifies the *bias* of each strategy form. It is the source for gains or losses and is determined arithmetically, short from long. The net investment position of the 130/30 strategy is 100. Its bias is positive.

For example: One can determine that the net investment position of the 25/75 strategy is -50 by subtracting the number of shares in its short position, 75, from the number of shares in its long investment, 25.

The return performance resulting from the net investment position in a long/short strategy is not the same as the performance of a long investment (one with a long/short ratio of 100/0) with a share quantity equal to the long/short strategy's net investment position. Though the net investment position calculation for both may be equal, the returns from their managed performance can be dramatically different.

For example: A long investment provides no advantages when share prices fall. A managed long/short strategy provides the opportunity for share quantity increases through profit-taking from the short position. When short profits are applied to the long side of the long/short ratio through the addition of long shares that have been purchased at a lower price, the security's return trajectory is increased. This rebalancing process lowers an investment's cost basis. *Cost basis* is the average price at which shares of the same security are purchased.

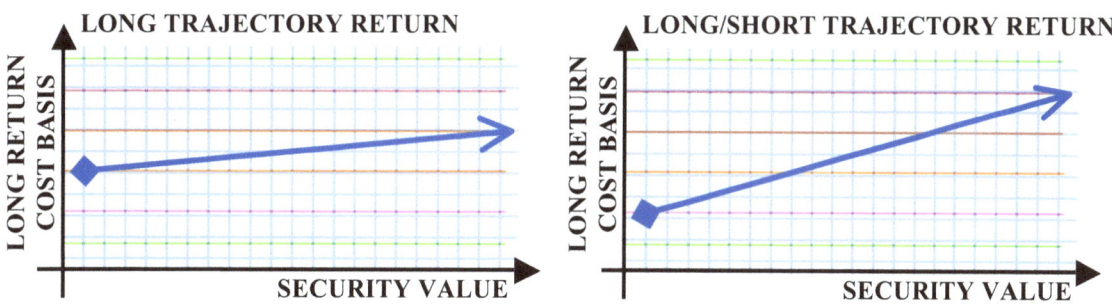

It is the opportunity to harvest profit from the winning side and to rebalance the investment position back to its original ratio with those harvested profits that makes long/short strategy hedging so lucrative in non-linear markets. A non-linear market is a market in which security prices move both up and down.

The differences among various long/short strategy forms and a long investment will be explained in this report, as will the opportunities for harvesting and stripping profit, and for increasing returns through leverage.

What Is A Long/Short Ratio?
Long identifies a type of trade. *Long* trades are purchased and held with the hope that securities values will appreciate so they can be sold later at a higher price. Long trades are investments. An *investment* is something bought.

Short trades are positions. A *position* is something sold. Short trades involve borrowing shares from a third party and selling them to the market with the hope that security values will depreciate so they can be purchased later at a lower price.

For example: A short trader borrows security shares from his broker to sell in the market at the current market price. This action opens the trade. The position trader expects that security share values will depreciate, so later he can close the trade by purchasing a set of comparable security shares at a price lower than that at which they were sold.

Long/Short is the name of a hedging strategy. The strategy simultaneously buys a quantity of security shares (long) and sells a quantity of security shares (short). The longs and shorts can be different securities or the same security.

One form of the Long/Short is called a *pair trade* (see page 20 for strategy explanation). Another form is called a *hedged box*. The hedged box is a market-neutral strategy. Two derivative based market neutral long/short strategies are known as the *straddle* and *strangle*. Derivatives can be used to boost returns through the intrinsic leverage that they provide when substituted for the primary securities on one or both sides of a hedging strategy.

Long/Short Ratio Strategy Definitions

(i) **Investment** is something purchased that creates a net outflow of monies.

(ii) **Position** is something sold that creates a net inflow of monies.

(iii) **Long** refers to an investment in a security; also a directional trade making market profits only when a security's market price rises.

(iv) **Short** refers to a position in a security; also a directional trade making market profits only when a security's market price falls.

(v) **ETFs (Exchange Traded Funds)** are equity securities that trade like stocks on a stock exchange. The ETF is composed of a basket of individual securities. Index ETFs seek to mimic an index by holding the group of stocks that compose the index in a proportion appropriate to cause price values of an index ETF to move in tandem with the actual index values to an accuracy (*correlation*) of 98% or greater.

Indices are the Dow Jones Industrial Average, Standard & Poor's 500, Nasdaq 100, Wilshire 1000 and Russell 2000, to name a few.

Index ETF prices are a fraction of their mimicked index. For example, the SPY is 1/10th the value of the Standard and Poor's 500 Index. If the Standard and Poor's 500 Index is 1000, the SPY will be trading at approximately $100.

6

By definition, indices are diversified, therefore Index ETFs are diversified. Index ETFs with ticker symbols like the SPY, DIA and QQQQ representing the Standard and Poor's 500 Index, the Dow Jones Industrial Average and the NASDAQ 100 experience high levels of daily trading volume.

(vi) **Backtracking** is a loss of price appreciation, value gains and profits caused by an adverse movement in the price and value of a security.

(vii) **Points Of Action Within A Long/Short Ratio Strategy**

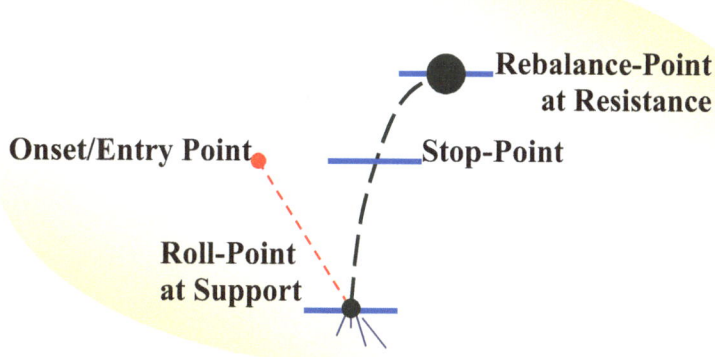

(a) Stop-point is the technically determined price at which the security will breakout through its moving average resistance level and then maintain a bullish trend.

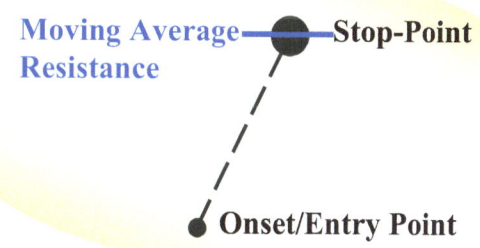

This stop-point can trigger the rebalancing of the investment position to a long/short ratio, with a greater positive bias and more bullish weight. Also, it can be the point at which the short position is closed, leaving only the long investment to profit as the security price continues its upward trend. A long investment share quantity value equal to the short position loss can be liquidated and combined with the onset short sale proceeds to discharge the total short side liability.

(b) Rebalance-point is the point at which the position and investment values are to be returned to the onset ratios, or equalized in a hedged box strategy after the security price has risen. This process is called rebalancing.

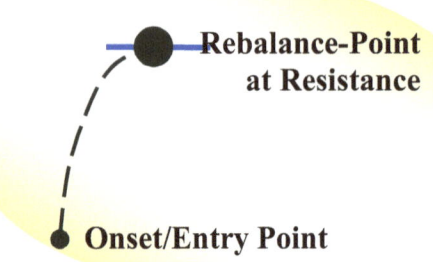

Rebalance-Point
at Resistance

Onset/Entry Point

Rebalancing resets the initial onset/entry point to the current higher security price, removing the need for price backtracking to the onset/entry point at which further price declines are needed to create short-side profit stripping opportunities. Any security price decline now will be rewarded with instant short-side profit stripping opportunities.

The long/short ratios can be rebalanced to the onset ratios without or with the addition of margin (see page 12 for an explanation of margin). The steps for rebalancing without the use of margin are:

> **Step 1:** sell a quantity value of long side security shares equal to the loss of value incurred by the short side after the security price rose from the onset/entry point to the current rebalance-point; then

> **Step 2:** simultaneously close (with combined proceeds from the onset short sale and the sale of long side security shares from step 1) and reopen the short side position.

For example: If a 150/50 Long/Short strategy is applied with a single security currently priced at $50, the value of the 150 long side shares is $7,500 (calculated as $50 multiplied by 150 security shares) and $2,500 for the short side shares (calculated as $50 multiplied by 50 security shares). When the security price rises from its onset price of $50 to $60, rebalancing the ratio without the addition of margin is accomplished by the following steps:

> **Step 1:** sell 8.33 long side security shares equaling $500, the total loss of value incurred by the short side when the price rose from the onset/entry point of $50 to the current rebalance-point of $60; then

Step 2: simultaneously close the current short position valued at $3,000 by purchasing the short shares from the market with sale proceeds of $2,500 from the onset transaction and $500 from step 1, and reopen a short side position by selling 47.22 shares, a value equal to the desired ratio now based on the rebalance-point long side value from step 1 of $8,500 (calculated as $9,000 minus $500).

The steps for rebalancing with the addition of margin are:

Step 1: simultaneously close and reopen the short-side position in the desired ratio, now based on the rebalance-point long side value; then

Step 2: use margin to cover the short side value loss resulting from security price appreciation from the onset/entry point to the rebalance point.

Value Based Rebalancing (Non-margined)	Share Based Rebalancing (Non-margined)
Onset/entry point values: long side = $7,500 short side = $2,500 **Rebalance-point values:** long side = $9,000 short side = $3,000 **Step 1:** **Rebalance-point values during rebalance:** long side = $8,500 short side = $3,000 **Step 2:** **Rebalance-point values after rebalance:** long side = $8,500 short side = $2,833.20	**Onset/entry point share count:** long side = 150 short side = 50 **Rebalance-point share count:** long side = 150 short side = 50 **Step 1:** **Rebalance-point share count during rebalance:** long side = 141.67 short side = 50 **Step 2:** **Rebalance-point share count after rebalance:** long side = 141.67 short side = 47.22

For example: If a 150/50 Long/Short strategy is applied with a single security currently priced at $50, the value of the 150 long side shares is $7,500 (calculated as $50 multiplied by 150 security shares) and $2,500 for the short side shares (calculated as $50 multiplied by 50 security shares). When the security price rises from its onset price of $50 to $60, rebalancing the ratio with the addition of margin is accomplished by the following steps:

Step 1: simultaneously buy back from the market 50 short shares at a security price of $60 and borrow to sell to the market 50 short shares at a security price of $60; then

Step 2: use margin of $500 to cover the short side value loss due as a result of the security share price movement from the onset-point of $50 to the rebalance-point of $60 (calculated as rebalance-point value of $3,000 from onset-point value of $2,500). Note that the overall profit/loss condition of this trade is a net gain of $1,000 (calculated as a long side gain of $1,500 and a short side loss of $500).

Value Based Rebalancing (Margined)	Share Based Rebalancing (Margined)
Onset/entry point values: long side = $7,500 short side = $2,500	**Onset/entry point share count:** long side = 150 short side = 50
Step 1 **Rebalance-point values** **prior to rebalance:** long side = $9,000 short side = $3,000	**Step 1** **Rebalance-point share count** **prior to rebalance:** long side = 150 short side = 50
Step 2 **Rebalance-point values** **after rebalance:** long = $9,000; short = $3,000; margin = $500	**Step 2** **Rebalance-point share count** **after rebalance:** long = 150 short = 50 margin = 8.33

When rebalancing a hedged box strategy with equal long side and short side share quantities, the new investment position value amounts after rebalancing without margin will always be equal to the original investment position value amounts at the onset/entry point. The difference is that fewer shares will be involved, because the security share price is now higher.

(c) Roll-point is the price point at which short position profits are stripped for the benefit of (i) skewing the bias of the investment position through the purchase of additional long shares, (ii) converting short side profits into cash, or (iii) unhedging the long side investment in anticipation of an upside price rebound.

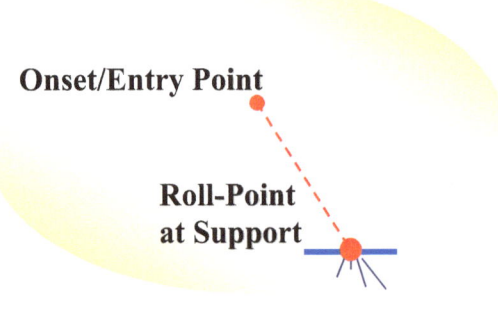

What Is A Hedge?

A *hedge* is an act, tool or means of preventing value loss in one security with another long or short partially or fully counter-balancing security. A hedge reduces the possibility of a loss of principal (value) due to adverse movements of the investment or position. If one security depreciates in value, the counter-balancing security will appreciate in value.

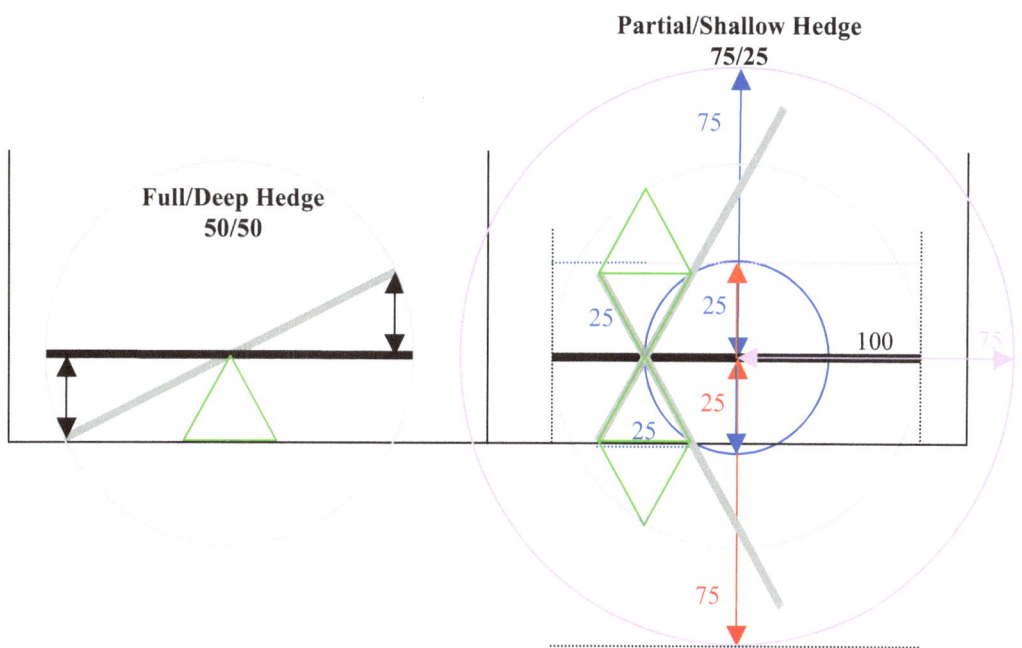

Hedging provides degrees of protection. When hedge protection is purchased, the more expensive the purchased protection, the greater the hedge. A hedge may be realized through purchases of counter-balancing securities as well as through sales of counter-balancing securities. The profit from one side of a hedged pair of securities may be harvested in a manner that continues to provide a hedge for the security pair. Profits from a hedged pair of securities may be harvested whenever available and supportive of the hedge.

The diagram above shows that a hedge is full, perfect, deep or counter-balancing, because there is no loss in value from security price movements. A shallow hedge experiences loss in value (in red) through an additive interpretation of price movements.

Perfectly hedged is the elimination of all risk. Risk is the possibility of loss in investment or position value. A perfectly hedged investment position that uses derivatives can make profit, but a perfectly hedged investment position of primary securities will not.

Primary securities are valued from actual supply and demand market forces. When the long/short strategy form of a perfectly hedged ratio uses only one primary security for both long and short sides, the losing side losses will be equal to the winning side gains.

Derivatives include two components in their valuation. One is definable security value derived from the primary security that values it and the other is speculative value. This speculative value component called *time value* is erratic, often not fully rational and subject to manipulation that can create profit harvesting opportunities.

In a down market, the profit from the winning short position is applied to the purchase of additional long units for the losing investment side, in anticipation of the inevitable market rebound.

What Is Margin?

Margin is something borrowed--borrowed money used to purchase security shares for a long trade or borrowed security shares to sell to the market as a short trade. Margin fees are charged by a brokerage on money borrowed to purchase security shares and on security shares when they are borrowed for the application of shorting. Long margin shares are identified by their value and short margin shares by their share quantity.

A *margin account* (interpret it as a borrowing account) is a trading account that allows the account owner to borrow money from the brokerage to purchase security shares (long) or to borrow security shares for sale to the market (short). The maximum amount that can be borrowed is 100% of the uncollateralized fully-owned cash amount in the account, or the amount equal to the value of the security shares that can be purchased (long) without margin.

Initial margin is the maximum dollar value or share amount that can be borrowed in a margin account. The initial margin criteria has been established by the Board of Governors of the United States Federal Reserve System under a regulation titled *Regulation T*. Rules for minimum margin have been agreed upon and formalized by the Securities and Exchange Commission, participating stock, forward and option exchanges, and broker-dealer self-regulating organizations.

Account equity is collateral for margin (the loan). *Equity* is the sum of uncollateralized and fully-owned cash and security shares. Security shares are valued at ½ their market value when considered a component of equity.

The *initial margin requirement* (interpret it as the amount of equity (collateral) required to gain initial margin) for trades of stocks and non-leveraged ETFs (ETFs that themselves do not employ leverage) is 50% in retail investor accounts; 25% in professional investor accounts (pattern day traders) and even less in market-makers and large balance accounts ($45 million) deemed exempt from the rules established by Regulation T.

Minimum margin (interpret it as minimum overnight margin) is the point to which the purchased (long) margined security value can fall, or the short sale (short) margined share value can rise, that will make the account equity (collateral) insufficient to comfortably collateralize margin (the loan).

Minimum margin requirement (interpret it as the amount of equity needed to keep a margin account in good standing) for stocks and non-leveraged ETFs purchased (long) on margin is 25%; 30% for these equity securities sold short on margin. Professional investors typically do not hold unhedged securities overnight, so there is no need to establish an additional minimum margin requirement percentage specifically for them. However, if the criteria are met, minimum margin requirement does exist in the form of *portfolio margin requirement*, which is based on potential and probable maximum loss predictions dictated by hedging activities called offsets.

Other rules apply, including margin guidelines for options, futures and bonds. Brokerages can establish more stringent rules beyond those established by Regulation T and margin rules, including requirements for higher account balances, higher initial margin levels and higher minimum margin levels.

Margin Calculations

Security share values fluctuate over the holding period of a trade. Account equity is the gauge for margin account health. Margin calculations are exclusive to each margin trade, though exceptions exist. Accounts with multiple margin trades consider margin account health additively for each trade equity calculation. If initial margin is established at the 50% level, a margin account with $4,000 of beginning equity (in the form of cash) can control $8,000 in share value. Trade equity of a margined investment is determined by the formula:

> **Share Value Of The Trade − Amount Borrowed = Equity**
>
> commonly written as
>
> **Market Value − Margin = Equity**

The share value of each trade includes what is purchased on margin (with borrowed money) and with equity (cash). Share value fluctuations are reflected only in account equity, never in the amount borrowed, which remains constant until repaid. The collateral for margin is the market value of the shares purchased with both margin and equity.

The minimum margin requirement for investment trades in margin accounts is account equity value of 25% the current share value of the trade. Since 200 shares at $40 are purchased using a cash base of $4,000, the minimum price to which shares can drop before being in violation of margin rules is $26.66, calculated as:

> PRELIMINARY CALCULATION
> **Share Price × Initial Margin Percentage = Total Margin Amount Per Share**
> $40 × 50% = $20
>
> CALCULATION
> **Total Margin Amount Per Share ÷ (1 − Minimum Margin Requirement)**
> $20 ÷ (1 − 25%)
> $26.66

Where at the onset of the trade the account reflects an equity value of $4,000, the account equity calculation for a margin account is:

> **Total Share Value Of All Trades − Amount Borrowed = Account Equity**
> $8,000 − $4,000 = $4,000

With a decline in share price to $26.66, the account reflects an equity value of $1,332.

> **($26.66 x 200) − $4,000 = $1,332**

$1,332 is 25% the current total share value ($5,332) of the trade(s) at a share price of $26.66 for 200 shares.

A margin call will be issued if share prices fall below the $26.66 threshold. Cash in an amount equal to the deficit account equity amount must be deposited to make equity at least 25% the current share value of the account. Or fully-owned, non-obligated and non-collateralized equity security shares twice the value of the deficit account equity amount can be deposited or combined with cash to eliminate the deficit equity amount.

Trade account equity of a margined position short sale is determined by the formula:

$$\textbf{(Initial Cash Deposit + Total Short Sale Proceeds)} - \textbf{Share Value Of The Trade} = \textbf{Equity}$$

The initial cash deposit (collateral) and the short sale proceeds from the short sale are not affected by share value fluctuations and remain constant until the position is closed, the same as the amount borrowed (margin) figure from the margined investment trade formula (page 14).

The minimum margin requirement for short equity security trades in margin accounts is account equity of 30% the current total share value of the trade. Since 200 shares at $40 are sold short from a cash base of $4,000, the maximum price to which the shares can rise before being in violation of margin rules is $46.15, calculated as:

$$\textbf{(Initial Cash Deposit + Total Short Sale Proceeds)} \div \textbf{(1 + Minimum Margin Requirement))} \div \textbf{Total Shares Sold Short}$$
$$\textbf{(\$12,000} \div \textbf{(1 + 30\%))} \div \textbf{200}$$
$$\textbf{\$9,230.77} \div \textbf{200}$$
$$\textbf{\$46.15}$$

When at the onset of the trade the account reflects an equity value of $4,000, the margin account formula is:

$$\textbf{(Initial Cash Deposit + Total Short Sale Proceeds)} - \textbf{Share Values Of Account} = \textbf{Equity}$$
$$\textbf{(\$4,000 + \$8,000)} - \textbf{\$8,000} = \textbf{\$4,000}$$

With a rise in share price to $46.15, the account reflects an equity value of $2,770.

$$(\$4,000 + \$8,000) - (\$46.15 \times 200) = \$2,770$$

$2,770 is 30% the current share value ($9,230) of the trade at a share price of $46.15 for 200 shares.

A margin call will be issued if equity share prices rise above the $46.15 threshold. Cash in an amount equal to the deficit account equity amount must be deposited to make account equity at least 30% the current share value of the account. Or fully-owned, non-obligated and non-collateralized equity security shares twice the value of the deficit account equity amount can be deposited or combined with cash to eliminate the deficit equity amount.

The Margined Short Sale Position Versus The Margined Long Investment
The short sale position is based on share quantity, unlike the long investment, which is based on dollar value. Security shares are the position trader's liability. Dollars are the investor's liability.

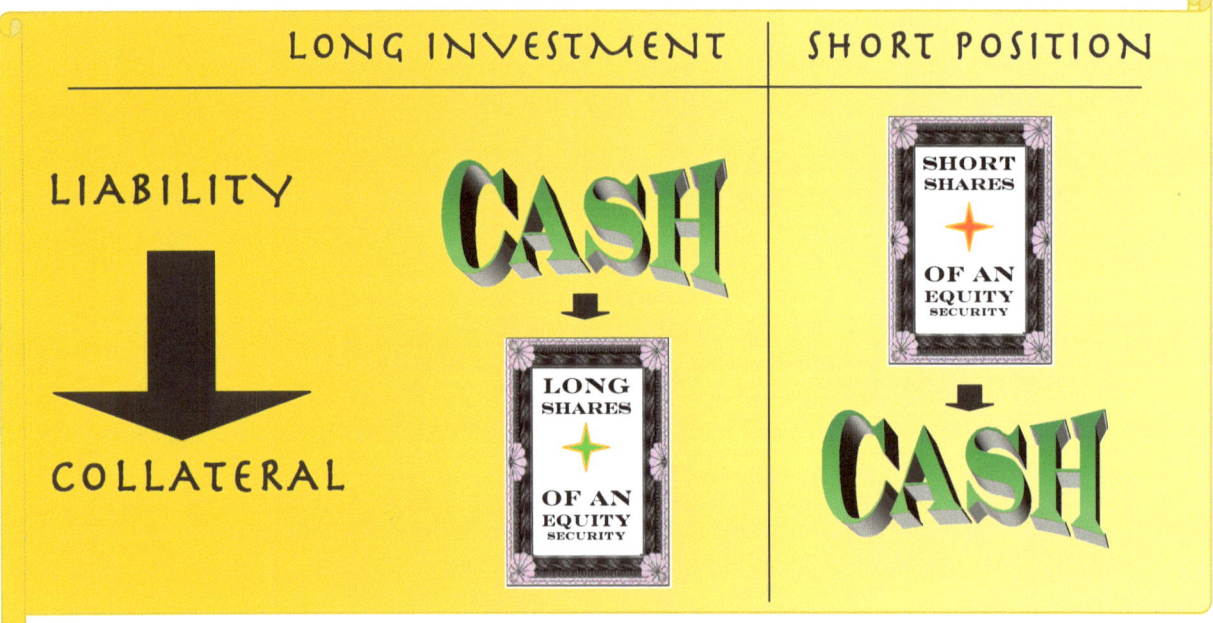

The short trader transacts a short sale by margining (borrowing) shares and selling them to the market at prevailing market prices. The collateral for the short margin is the cash proceeds from the short sale. This collateral (the cash) can not be used for any other purpose.

The long investor leverages an investment by margining dollars to buy additional shares. The long margin liability of dollars is converted (collateralized) into security shares when the investor leverages the investment by purchasing additional shares. This collateral (the shares) cannot be used for any other purpose.

What Is Leverage?

Leverage is the process of using margin to control an investment or position that is larger than what could be controlled with account equity alone. Leverage is not free. A cost is assessed daily in the form of interest on the total amount margined. Leverage produces yield, a higher return than can be created without the use of margin.

Yield is return calculated from the investment, position or investment position profit result of long or short security shares controlled with both equity and margin, divided by account equity (the portion of an investment, position, or investment position not margined).

For example: Suppose that both investor *A* and investor *B* each have equity of $100. Investor *A* goes long (invests in) 100 $1 shares. If investor *A's* 100 shares appreciate 5% to close at an ending value of $105; $5 is investor *A's* total profit for a return of 5%. Margin will allow investor *B* to own 200 shares of that $1 security that appreciates 5% to $210 ($105 multiplied by 2); $10 is investor *B's* total profit for a return of 5%. The yield is 10% (calculated as $10, the overall profit from both non-margined and margined long shares, divided by $100, the equity amount used to establish the leveraged trade). This example does not consider the margin costs.

For example: The market has priced shares of an equity security at $40. A margin account has a cash balance of $4,000.

> *How much value of this security can an investor purchase (long) on margin?*
> The maximum amount is twice the cash balance; $8,000 (calculated as $4000 × 2 = $8,000)

> *How many shares of this security can an investor sell short (short) on margin?*
> The maximum share value amount is twice the cash balance; 200 shares (calculated as $4000 × 2 = $8,000; $8,000 ÷ $40 = 200 shares).

At what point does margin use become unwise?

The return on margin calculation provides the answer. The annualized return on margin calculation is slightly different from the annualized return calculation because it focuses its value analysis on only the long and short amounts borrowed, instead of on the total monies used in the trade. If the returns provided from borrowing exceed the costs to borrow, leveraging through margin is a justifiable practice and expense. Annualized return on margin is determined by the formula:

$$(((\text{Final Balance} - \text{Initial Balance}) \div \text{Amount Borrowed}) + 1)^{(1 \div (\text{trade duration} \div 365))} - 1$$

How many shares of a security can an investor simultaneously long and short in a brokerage account?

Brokerages do not allow a retail trader to hold shares of the same security long and short in a margin account at the same time.

This rule places the retail trader at a disadvantage on two counts. The first and most significant disadvantage is that the opportunity to earn a position return from a long/short ratio strategy trade during a security price decline is lost. The second disadvantage is that the opportunity to protect long term investment profits from adverse price movements without incurring a taxable sale at the end of bullish price action is lost (provided the IRS Publication 550 rule criteria for not incurring capital gains taxes is met (see page 34)).

The retail trader's workaround solution for this disadvantageous rule is to open a second margin account at the same or a different brokerage. One account will be for long margin trades (the first half of the long/short ratio) and the second account will be for short margin trades (the second half of the long/short ratio).

A trader can benefit from a concurrent short position on the same security held as an investment. Using the same security on both long and short sides eliminates security specific inefficiencies created from security share price manipulation.

Mating Correlation

When brokerages disallow use of same security long/short investment positions, the alternative is to mate securities that are nearly correlated with a correlation variable approaching 100% or 1. The *correlation* variable is a measure of the consistency with which two securities move in the same direction, by the same percentage, at the same time.

The following example charts two equity index securities with a correlation coefficient of .99 (nearly perfect). As a consequence of their high correlation and their component securities, these ETFs both have beta (β) values equal to .97. The beta value of the overall market measured by any of the major market indices is equal to 1.

Reproduced with permission of Yahoo, Inc. (c)2010 Yahoo! Inc. YAHOO and the YAHOO logo are registered trademarks of Yahoo, Inc.

Correlation coefficients approaching −100% or −1 identify securities that are mirror opposites. The ETFs for the short US dollar (UDN) and the long US dollar (UUP) are good examples of negative correlation. Though negatively correlated to near perfection, the betas of these securities, 63.79 for UDN and −60.63 for UUP, differ from each other in an absolute sense by roughly 5%, at time of writing.

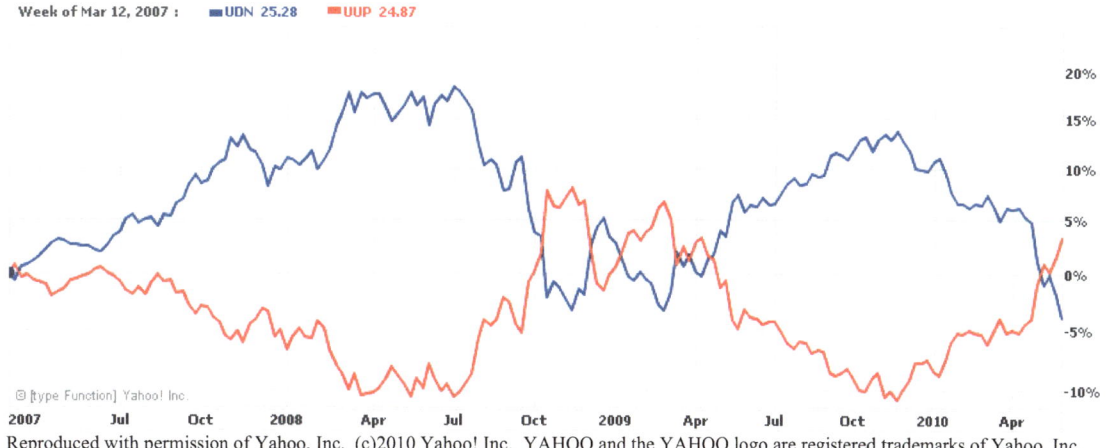

Reproduced with permission of Yahoo, Inc. (c)2010 Yahoo! Inc. YAHOO and the YAHOO logo are registered trademarks of Yahoo, Inc.

Betas and correlation coefficients change over time. A margin account is required to make a short sale. Trading accounts that do not qualify for margin status can approach the intent of the long/short strategy with two negatively correlated long equity securities such as the UDN and UUP.

If unable to determine the outright correlation between two securities, a loose approximation can be made with the statistical variable beta (β). Beta provides an indication of security specific price movements in relation to overall market movements. Since each security's beta is an analytical comparison between the market as a whole and itself, and not between two mated securities that are attempting to match correlation, tracking errors can occur when using beta for this purpose.

Reproduced with permission of Yahoo, Inc. (c)2010 Yahoo! Inc. YAHOO and the YAHOO logo are registered trademarks of Yahoo, Inc.

For example: The graph above shows the correlation between two securities with equal betas of .97. The correlation variable between these equity securities is −.37, a negative correlation, which is the result of securities tending toward opposite movements.

The Long/Short Pair Trade Strategy

A trader selects shares of a troubled company to short and shares of a strong company to long. If the market falls, it is hoped that the shorted shares of the troubled company will fall faster than the long shares of the stronger company. Likewise, if the market rises, the shorted shares of the troubled company will rise slower than the long shares of the stronger company.

Market sentiment is used to assist in the selection of a long/short ratio pair trade. The pair trade ratio is determined by investment value to position value (the value result is calculated by multiplying share quantities by share prices), not by share prices alone. Ratios can be 100/100 (not the same as 50/50, which represents a perfect risk-free hedge;

see page 11) for a market with no definite direction, or biased to favor current market conditions. Profit opportunities come from widening (increasing) long/short spread values and from long security dividend income.

The Greek symbol beta (β) suggests the degree a security moves up or down in relation to the market as a whole. A beta of 1 suggests that the percentage move of a security is exactly equal to the percentage move of the market. A beta of .90 suggests that the security will move on average 90% of the market's percentage movement in the same direction. A beta of 2.50 or greater suggests that the security is volatile and will move on average two and a half times the percentage movement of the market in the same direction.

The securities of weak or troubled companies are expected to have lower betas in rising markets and higher betas in falling markets. Betas are not constant over bull and bear market conditions.

For example: Company **H** has a strong public image and is experiencing increases in quarterly net income. Company **O** was discovered to be polluting the environment and now is experiencing decreases in quarterly net income. The product that companies **H** and **O** sell is a homogeneous (essentially alike) commodity.

A long/short pair trade buys the stock of company **H** and shorts the stock of company **O**. When the market rises, the share value of company **H** is expected to rise by a beta factor of 1.20. The share value of company **O** is expected to rise by a beta factor of .85. The value difference between the long and the short securities is the spread. A spread is profitable when its value increases (widens) from opening trade to closing trade.

SHORT-SIDE
INITIAL SHARE
VALUE: $48
BULL BETA: .85
BEAR BETA: 1.30

LONG-SIDE
INITIAL SHARE
VALUE: $40
BULL BETA: 1.20
BEAR BETA: 1.20

Note: The price of a security share has no bearing on the quality of a company when compared to the security share prices of other companies. Share price becomes a variable in determining company health only when compared to itself over time, not when compared to the share prices of other companies in the same industry. The fact that company **O** has a share price higher than company **H** means only that company **O**'s shares can fall in value $8 dollars farther than company **H**'s shares.

For example: The spread between company **H** and company **O** widened by $.58 as its closing value increased from −$8.00 (calculated as short security value, (−$48) from long security value ($40)) to −$7.42 (calculated as short security value (−$51.26) from long security value ($43.84)).

Another way of observing how spreads becomes profitable is to consider the money flow values from the time the pair trade is initiated or opened to the time the pair trade is closed.

OPENING TRANSACTION		CLOSING TRANSACTION	
BUY THE LONG	($40.00)	SELL THE LONG	$43.84
SELL THE SHORT	$48.00	BUY THE SHORT	($51.26)
TOTAL MONEY FLOW IN	$8.00	TOTAL MONEY FLOW OUT	($7.42)

In order to hold a long investment, the trader must debit (lower) cash reserves. That is why in the opening transaction the "buy the long" money flow is −$40. $40 is transferred out in exchange for the long security shares. To hold a short position, the trader receives cash because shares are sold first to open a short trade before they are purchased at a later time to close the trade. That is why in the opening transaction the "sell the short" money flow is +$48. Overall, the money that came in, $8.00, is more than the money that went out, -$7.42, making this a profitable trade as the market moved higher, illlustrated by the following diagram.

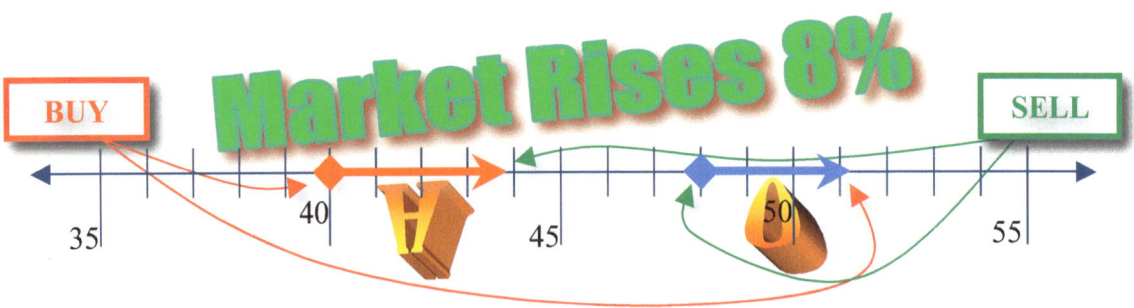

Assuming that supply and demand market forces do not influence security price action, the market rises 8% over the pair trade holding period. The initial share value of company **H** is $40; its ending share value is $43.84 (calculated as the 8% market return percentage multiplied by the bull market security beta of 1.20, multiplied by its $40 initial value). The initial share value of company **O** is $48; its ending share value is $51.26 (calculated as the 8% market return percentage multiplied by the bull market security beta of .85, multiplied by its $48 initial value).

The percentage increase in share values for this trading pair is 9.60% for company **H** and 6.79% for company **O**. The difference is 2.81% in favor of the long side, making this a profitable trade as anticipated by the behavior of these securities per their respective beta values.

Consider this long/short pair trade example in a falling market. Assuming that supply and demand market forces do not influence security price action, the market falls 7% over the holding period. The initial share value of company **H** is $40; its ending share value is $36.64 (calculated as the 7% market loss percentage multiplied by the bear market security beta of 1.20, multiplied by its $40 initial value). The initial share value of company **O** is $48; its ending share value is $43.63 (calculated as the 7% market loss percentage multiplied by the bear market security beta of 1.30, multiplied by its $48 initial value).

OPENING TRANSACTION		CLOSING TRANSACTION	
BUY THE LONG	($40.00)	SELL THE LONG	$36.64
SELL THE SHORT	$48.00	BUY THE SHORT	($43.63)
TOTAL MONEY FLOW IN	$8.00	TOTAL MONEY FLOW OUT	($6.99)

The spread between company **H** and company **O** widened by $1.01 as its closing value increased over its opening value of −$8 (calculated as short security value, (−$48) from long security value ($40) to −$6.99 (calculated as short security value (−$43.63) from long security value ($36.64)). The money that came in, $8.00, is more than the money that went out, −$6.99, making this a profitable trade as the market moved lower, illustrated in the diagram and chart on page 23.

The percentage decrease in share values for this trading pair is 8.40% for company **H** and 9.10% for company **O**. The difference is 0.70% in favor of the short side, making this a profitable trade as anticipated by the behavior of these securities per their respective beta values.

The long/short pair trade strategy produces a weak hedge. The trader plays both sides of the market, but profits only if two assumptions hold true:
1. When the market falls, the shorted security shares depreciate in value more than the long security shares.
2. When the market rises, the shorted security shares appreciate in value less than the long security shares.

If one of these assumptions does not hold true, the trader can make no profit or can suffer a loss.

The following report sections test and observe long/short ratio hedging strategies with the same security instead of with different securities.

Long/Short Ratio Descriptions
A trader can simultaneously margin long value and short shares in any ratio as long as investment and position values do not exceed twice the equity (cash) value.

For example: The market has priced shares of a security at $40. A margin account has a cash balance of $4,000. The following chart shows the possible configuration of some long/short ratios at maximum margin.

Long Shares	Short Shares	NIP**	Long/Short Ratio	Bias
200	0	200	---	+
160	40	120	160/40 (25% downside hedge)	+
150	50	100	150/50 (33% downside hedge)	+
100	100	0	50/50 (flat - 100% hedge)	---
50	150	-100	50/150 (33% upside hedge)	−
25	175	-150	25/175 (14% upside hedge)	−
0	200	-200	---	−

**NIP is net investment position

The following chart shows some long/short ratios at partial margin with a reserve of cash.

Long Shares	Shorted Shares	NIP**	Long/Short Ratio	Bias	Cash
130	30	100	130/30 (23% downside hedge)	+	20%
120	20	100	120/20 (17% downside hedge)	+	30%
80	20	60	80/20 (25% downside hedge)	+	50%
40	80	-40	40/80 (50% upside hedge)	−	40%
25	75	-50	25/75 (33% upside hedge)	−	50%

**NIP is net investment position

Note that the 130/30 and 120/20 ratios have the same net investment position, but the 120/20 requires less money on margin. The tradeoff is that a security price move against the bias of the 130/30 ratio will be countered with a hedge that is 6% higher than the hedge of the 120/20 ratio.

80/20 Long/Short Ratio Strategy

Example: The price of an equity security is $20 in an unleveraged 80/20 long/short ratio strategy with its ratio based on share quantity, not share value. 80 security shares are purchased (invested). 20 security shares are borrowed and sold short to the market (positioned). The net investment position is 60. The bias is positive.

The long value is $1,600 (calculated as 80 security shares multiplied by the $20 share price). The short share quantity value is $400 (calculated as 20 security shares multiplied by the $20 share price).

A short position becomes profitable to the trader when the security share value falls. If the security share price falls from $20 to $15, the long value will be $1,200 and the short share quantity value will be $300. The profit/loss on this 80/20 long/short ratio trade is a loss of $400 on the 80 share investment and a profit of $100 on the 20 share position. The net is a loss of $300.

The $100 position profit can be stripped by purchasing all of the short shares from the market at a price lower than that at which they were sold. Remember the truism "buy low and sell high" to make profit. It also applies to the short sale process. The difference is that the steps are reversed.

Continuing the facts in the example, use the $100 short sale profit to purchase (long) 6 additional security shares (calculated as the profit of $100 divided by $15 (the current security share price), which is 6.67). This boosts the current long value from $1,200 to $1,290 (calculated as the additional 6 long security shares (fractional share quantity of .67 discarded in this share quantity based example) multiplied by $15 (the current security share price), plus the current value of the 80 long security shares).

The 80/20 long/short ratio still must be maintained (based on share quantity in this example, not value), so if 86 shares are now 80 of the ratio, 21.5 short shares must be sold to become 20 of the ratio (calculated as 86 long shares divided by 80, multiplied by 20; fractional share quantity of .5 discarded).

If the security share price rises from $15 to $21, the long value appreciates to $1,816 and the short share quantity value rises to $441. A short position becomes profitable to the trader only when the security share value falls, the profit/loss on this 80/20 long/short trade from the $15 security share roll-point reset is a profit of $526 on the 86 security share investment and a loss of $126 on the 21 security share position. Adding this second round result (the rise from $15 to $21) for both the long investment and the short position to the first round result (the drop from $20 to $15) determines that the 80/20 long/short strategy trade with a stripping of short profit, and rebalancing of 6 added shares to the long side at a $15 security price, produced an overall profit of $90.00.

The 80/20 long/short strategy cost basis of the long shares was lowered from $20.00 per share to $19.65 per share when short side profits were stripped and used to increase the long investment share count from 80 to 86. The short side position was reset to a share count of 21 to maintain the approximate 25% hedge of the 80/20 ratio if the security share price declined again (24.41% considering that fractional shares were discarded).

Ratios can be established based on share quantity or share value. There will be a slight difference in favor of share value ratios when comparing returns, because fractional share quantity reserves are not put into service with share quantity based ratios. A share value ratio in the form of the 80/20 is 80% investment value long to 20% position value short. A share quantity ratio in the form of the 80/20 is exactly 80 shares long to exactly 20 shares short.

For example: Placing an unleveraged account equity amount equal to $3,583 into service using an 80/20 share quantity ratio on an equity security with a market price of $26 puts 109 long shares and 27 short shares into service. The 109 long and 27 short shares count of this 80/20 ratio equals a share quantity value of $3,536. The difference from $3,583 to $3,536 is fractional share quantity reserves (unused equity), because security shares are traded only as wholes, not as fractions. If there is a 2% value appreciation on total equity used, the profit based on share quantity value ($3,536) will be $70.72, but the profit based on fully used equity ($3,583) will be $71.66.

The Unleveraged Long/Short Ratio Versus The Long Investment
Hedging is not without its drawbacks. Opponents of long/short ratio trading argue that the opportunity cost of unhindered long only returns is limited by a long/short ratio's counterbalancing position losses, making long/short ratio strategies ineffective.

Proponents of long/short ratio trading argue that security prices do not always appreciate, so it is advantageous to profit in some degree when the market is backtracking, by using position profits to purchase and add lower cost security shares to the long side, which increases the investment trajectory by reducing the investment side cost basis and increasing the appreciating share quantity.

Compare the results of an 80/20 long/short ratio strategy with those of a long investment using a trade equity value of $2,000, rather than a net investment position value of 60. The onset/entry point is $20, the roll-point is $15 and the final value is $21. The non-profit-rolling result favors the long investment by $40, $2100 versus $2060.

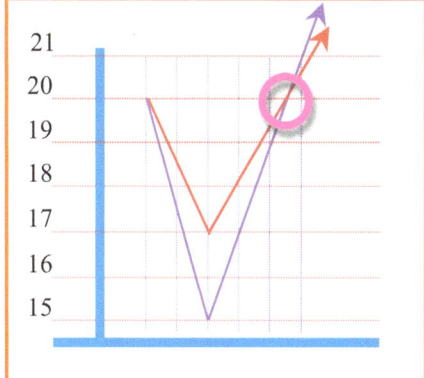

COMPARED VIA AN EQUAL
INVESTMENT EQUITY VALUE
OF $2,000, NON-PROFIT-ROLLING

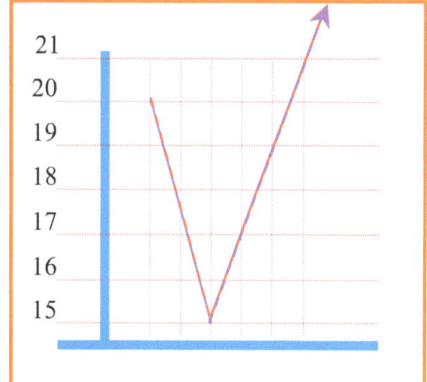

COMPARED VIA AN EQUAL
NET INVESTMENT POSITION
OF 60, NON-PROFIT-ROLLING

A LEVERAGED 120/20 LONG/SHORT RATIO COMPARED VIA AN EQUAL NET INVESTMENT POSITION OF 100

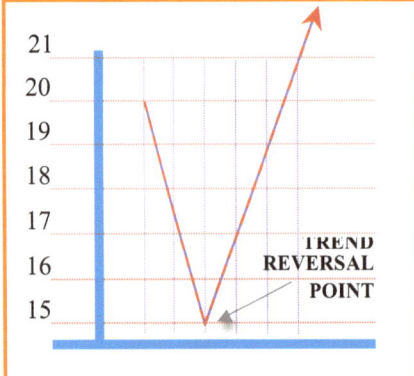

A LEVERAGED 120/20 LONG/SHORT RATIO WITH PROFIT ROLLING AT $15 COMPARED VIA AN EQUAL NIP

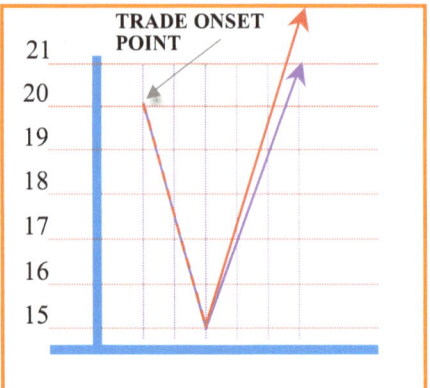

Equal trade equity values favor the long investment (purple line in the first graph on the prior page) after the comparison crossing point (pink circle). Equal net investment position values favor the long/short ratio strategy (maroon line in the graphs above) throughout the life of the trade with one roll placed anywhere after and between the trend reversal point and the onset trade point.

The opportunity to strip short side profits makes a significant difference in profit and return when compared to a trading strategy with no price decline profit stripping opportunity, as is the case in a long only trade.

Long/short traders use leverage to boost the net investment position of their long/short ratios to 100. This ensures that long/short ratio return results (less margin and trading fees) always outperform those of the benchmark, a long investment.

The 130/30 Versus The 150/50 Long/Short Margin Ratio Hedge Strategy
The 130/30 is a ratio description of a portfolio or strategy structure, and refers to the number of shares long (130) to the number of shares short (30). Leverage is employed to attain these cumulative ratio values in excess of 100.

The 130/30 Long/Short Margin Ratio Hedge strategy provides a dependable downside hedge of 23% when using the same security. By comparison, the 150/50 Long/Short Margin Ratio Hedge strategy provides a dependable downside hedge of 33%.

Why one long/short ratio over the other? It is a matter of market sentiment. If the market is trending in a bullish manner, the ratio with the higher net investment position will outperform the ratio with a lower net investment position.

For example: If less bullish and more bearish, the 150/50 rather than the 130/30 will be applied, because the 150/50 establishes 33% of the investment position to be profitable in a down market, compared to 23% of the investment position with the 130/30.

If the belief is that the market sentiment will remain very bullish and prolonged backtracking or the need for downside protection is not a major concern, the better long/short ratio is the 130/30. The 130/30 requires less leverage and provides a net investment position equal to that of the 150/50.

Both strategies have a net investment position equal to 100. The 130/30 achieves this by borrowing less money. It has 10% less downside protection than the 150/50. The number of shares leveraged in the 150/50 ratio is 100 (calculated as 100 subtracted from the ratio sum of long and short shares). The number of shares leveraged in the 130/30 is 60. When long side trajectories are constant, the 130/30 gives the same upside performance as the 150/50 with less leverage and margin cost.

Market Sentiment Insight From The Technical Indicator VIX

The most important component for achieving success on all long/short strategies is a market condition that produces high price action measured as the percentage and the quantity of price moves within a given trading period. Together these components are called volatility. The best measure for whole market volatility is the derivative VIX.

The Chicago Board Options Exchange (CBOE) introduced the symbol VIX, as the measure of volatility for the S&P 100 index in 1993. It was applied to the S&P 500 Index in 2003. Though typically read as a measure for possible market declines, the VIX can also signal the movement up of market prices.

Valuable insight into the anticipated amplitude of near-term security share prices can be acquired if the beta variable of a security is known. Combining (multiplying) the beta variable of a security with the VIX-predicted percentage price movement results of the S&P 500 Index can suggest a security trading range that has a 68% chance of occurring.

Applying an additional calculation to the VIX reading will determine the 30-day anticipated price movement (range) percentage for the S&P 500 index. That resulting percentage movement can be up, down, or a range composed of both up and down movements. The calculation produces a possible percentage price movement, within the following 30 days, that has a 68% chance of occurring.

The chart to the right shows possible percentage price movements for the S&P 500 index in the right column when the VIX returns the following values in the left column.

	15	4.33%	
Average	19.04	5.50%	1990 - October 2008
	20	5.77%	
	40	11.55%	
	60	17.32%	
	80	23.09%	
High	89.53	25.85%	October 24, 2008

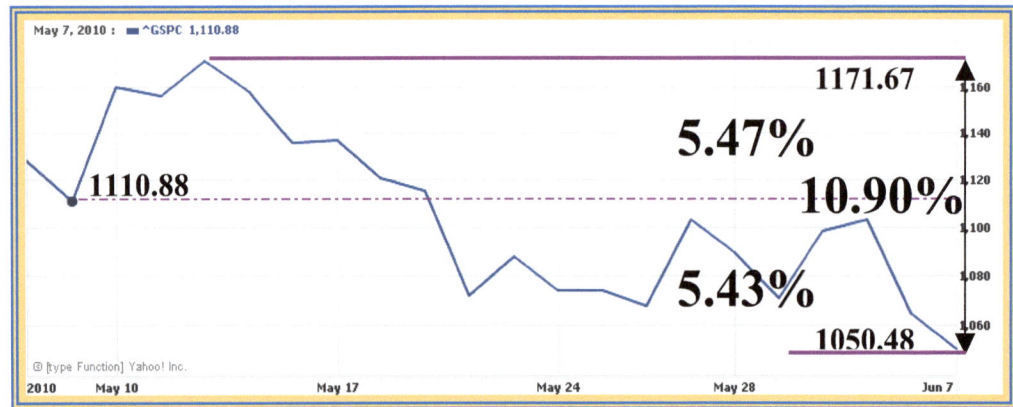

May 7, 2010 : ^GSPC 1,110.88

1171.67

5.47%

10.90%

1110.88

5.43%

1050.48

Reproduced with permission of Yahoo, Inc. (c)2010 Yahoo! Inc. YAHOO and the YAHOO logo are registered trademarks of Yahoo, Inc.

The graph above plots the S&P 500 index from May 7th to June 7th, 2010. The May 7 VIX closing value of 40.95 is observed for predictive accuracy. The 40.95 VIX value suggests that there is a 68% chance that there will be price movement in the S&P 500 index by 11.84%, up, down or in combination within the following 30 days.

As predicted, the S&P 500 index moved dramatically by high percentages in both directions. Combined, the maximum range in the 30 day period between May 7th to June 7th was 10.90%. The VIX based price movement calculation was off by only 8% from the actual; a grade of A, 92 out of 100.

Exploitable Security Inefficiencies
Determining market sentiment and using it to time entry and exit into a single company's security shares is difficult. One reason market timing on company shares is difficult is because of trading inefficiencies; specifically the manipulation of security share prices.

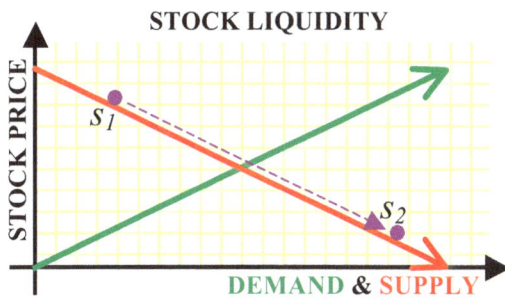

The practice of short selling increases the liquidity (supply) of an equity security. Basic economic tenets demonstrate that the price of an equity security falls when there is greater supply.

Short sellers form trading pools directly (illegally) and indirectly (legally) to raid the price of equity securities by repeatedly short selling them.

Rule 10a-1 was adopted by the Securities and Exchange Commission in 1938 to combat this manipulative behavior. The rule was called the "Up-Tick Rule" and required that short sales occur only after the last transaction (or the transaction before it in the event that there was no price change) is an increase in share price (an up-tick) rather than a decrease in share price. On July 6, 2007, the "Up-tick Rule" was eliminated, allowing short sellers the opportunity to strip value from equity shares lent by the mutual funds of pensioners, insurance trusts and retirees.

Eliminating the "Up-tick Rule" was not the cause of the 2008-2009 market crash and recession. But it more than likely encouraged the furious pace at which market values plummeted in the period from September through October, 2008 (**red** rectangle).

The results are hard to miss.

The stock market experiences stock manipulation daily, most noticeably at opening bell when a stock opens in one direction, then quickly moves in the other direction. This would not occur if stock trading were an efficient event. The daily trajectory of stock price movements at the market open would remain consistent until events in the form of stock specific and market specific news influenced changes in direction through a consensus change in sentiment.

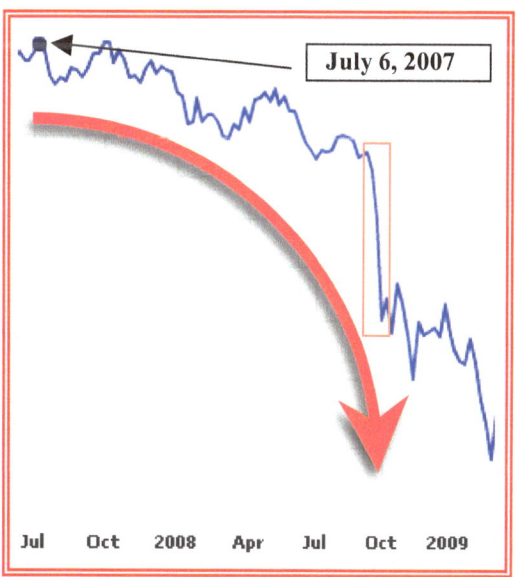

Reproduced with permission of Yahoo, Inc. (c)2010 Yahoo! Inc. YAHOO and the YAHOO logo are registered trademarks of Yahoo, Inc.

Until stock trading is made efficient, the only way to gain a trading advantage is through the use of hedging.

Trading and market efficiency depends on two inclusive factors:
1. The equal access to accurate information for all market participants.
2. The diversification of portfolio holdings to smooth portfolio value movements, removing the effect that security specific inefficiencies have on a portfolio return.

This first factor will never occur. It is common for executives to order the direct misrepresentation of their company's financial condition in accounting statements. They lie because their compensation is based on the share price appreciation of their company's stock. Balance sheets can not be trusted to provide an accurate representation of a company's financial strength. This means that fundamental analysis, the valuation of a stock through interpretation of a company's financial data to discover current and future values, is an invalid form of data interpretation for use in stock selection. Value investing uses the fundamental analysis methodology. Mutual funds or investment managers who call themselves practitioners of the value investing methodology should be engaged with caution.

The second factor for developing trading and market efficiency is achievable through the use of derivatives that attempt to mimic the market as a whole through index matching. These derivatives are index futures, index options and index ETFs (exchange traded funds). All are by definition fully diversified.

Ultimately, market efficiency is not possible. Market inefficiencies can benefit a trader using long/short ratio strategies. A trader using long/short ratio strategies on equity securities is playing both sides of the market. The trader depends on two truths to make long/short ratio hedging lucrative:
1. The mid-term market and the equity security trend (move) in the direction equal to the bias of the long/short ratio.
2. The trader can time market and security price movements, rebalancing profits from the winning side (investment or position) and increasing value or share count of that losing side in anticipation of a change in trend (also referred to as *harvesting profit from the long* or *stripping profit from the short)*.

The practice of harvesting or stripping profit attempts to keep value gains on the winning side through rebalancing. Proper rebalancing ensures that profits will remain in a state of continuous value growth. Long/short ratio strategies facilitate this.

Knowing when the market will reverse... is much harder than knowing if it has.

Stripping Profits

A roll-point will always be below the security price point at the onset of an investment position. It represents a fall in security share value. The short position will gain at the roll-point; the long position will lose.

Position gains can be stripped from the margined short shares to rebalance short side profits: (i) to the long side to discharge long side margin loss liabilities, (ii) to purchase additional shares to increase the ratio's net investment position, or (iii) to hold as cash. Stripping is accomplished by closing the short position to discharge its margin liability through a purchase of a share quantity equal to that which was borrowed and sold at the onset of the position trade. The short position can be reestablished (reset) by borrowing and selling a second set of security shares at the current market price. The process of reestablishing the short position switches old short security shares that have gained strippable profit for new short security shares.

Reestablishing short positions at the roll-point accomplishes three objectives:
1. Strips profit from the short position by purchasing shares at a security price lower than the price at which they are sold.
2. Returns borrowed shares to discharge the margin liability acquired when the short position was established.
3. When applied in the hedged box strategy (discussed on page 34), it maintains a short share position value equal to the long share investment value, fulfilling the requirements of the *hedged box rule* (NYSE Rule 431(e)(1)).

> NYSE Rule 431(e)(1) - When the same security is carried "long" and "short" the margin to be maintained on such positions [investment positions] shall be 5% of the current market value of the "long" securities. In determining such margin requirements "short" positions shall be marked to the market.

The Hedged Box, Risk Neutralizing Strategy

Boxed is a risk-neutralizing zero sum strategy. *Boxed, flattened* and *neutralized* are not the same as perfectly hedged. A perfectly hedged trade provides the opportunity for profit. A boxed trade provides no opportunity for profit.

A boxed trade can be used in the following circumstances:
1. The market is expected to crash.
2. Market sentiment is undeterminable.
3. The investment can not be monitored for an extended period of time.
4. A financial planner or investment advisor wishes to continue billing fees on a client's investments and would otherwise be unable to do so if the investments were liquidated to be held as cash in anticipation of adverse price movements.
5. An investor wishes to maintain investment gains for a period of time prior to their expected need, but does not wish to exit the investment now and incur a capital gains tax liability payable in the current tax year.

The caveat for use of a boxed trade in the fifth circumstance is that the investor must close the short side (position) of the box by purchasing it back from the market within 30 days of year-end in the year that the box was established. The investor must then maintain the investment for another 60 days without any form of identifiable hedge on the specific investment in order to avoid an assignment of tax liability accruing in the undesired year on the capital gains of the investment, measured at the security price point at which the box was established.

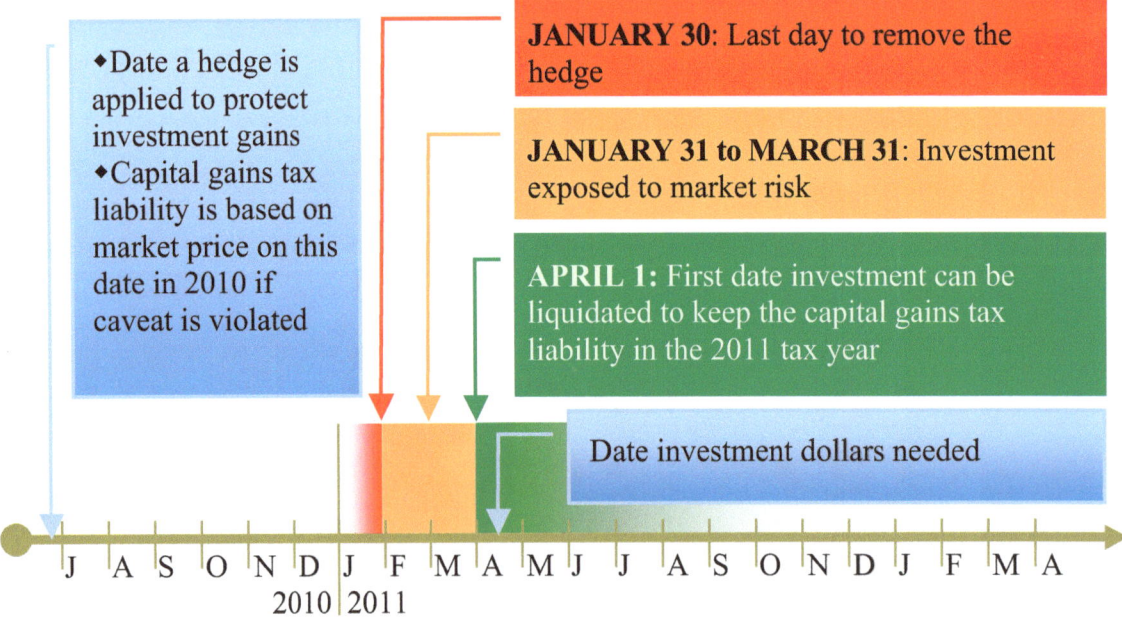

No matter what form an equity security long/short strategy takes, unlike derivative based long/short strategies, the only way it will produce a return is when at some point the hedge ratio is set to either a long or short bias. The hedged box strategy becomes profitable when the strategy bias shifts from its neutral state to either positive or negative. Stripped short profits must generate a positive return greater than trading costs and accruing margin fees. Otherwise, the hedged box equity security long/short strategy loses money.

Individual equity securities, sector ETFs, index ETFs, or bonds with high market specific price volatility, are *boxed* (in other words, *flattened* or *neutralized*, removing all possibility for loss due to adverse price movements) by holding an equal number of long securities (the investment) and short securities (the position).

The hedged box strategy nets gains and losses to zero. It protects from loss an investment or portfolio upon market entry when market sentiment is unknown or unpredictable. Money is placed equally on both the long and short sides of an equity security, creating a *market neutral* trade.

This strategy is an alternative to the dollar-cost-averaging entry method. *Direction specific profits* (realized in unhedged long investments or unhedged short positions) are increased through use of bias weighting and leverage once the market trend is determined.

Stripping Profit From The Hedged Box, Risk Neutralizing Strategy
If the market falls immediately upon entry with the hedged box strategy, profits are stripped from the winning side of the market (the short side) by buying back the short position at a price lower than it was sold. At this point the trader has two choices: (i) the short position only or both the short position and long investment can be discarded removing the trader from the market, or (ii) another short position equal to the current long investment value can be established to continue the offsetting characteristics of the box trade with the short stripped profits held as cash or used to apply a positive bias to the trade.

The stripped short side profit amount can be rebalanced through an allocating purchase of additional long security shares or a short sale of borrowed shares to skew the ratio bias from neutral to bearish. This breaks the hedge neutrality, which has been neither positive nor negative to this point. If a rebalance to long shares is selected in addition to a change in bias, the cost basis of the long shares can be lowered with the addition of lower cost security shares, raising the investment trajectory from its trade onset slope. The only way to profit from this point forward is if share price movements match the trade bias of the selected choice. If it does not, the strategy loses money.

The trader must be able to identify and time the trend bottom before he skews the investment position bias or employs leverage to boost returns, or he will accrue additional margin fees and losses while waiting for the security to match the strategy bias. Knowing that a security price trend has reversed is easier than knowing when it will reverse. A solid knowledge of technical analysis techniques is very valuable in timing strategy changes from a neutral bias to positive or negative

The process for stripping short side profits in a hedged box strategy to change the strategy bias to positive with no employed leverage is demonstrated in the following example.

For example: An equity security is priced at $10. 100 shares are boxed. The market sentiment is unknown. The trade occurs over two days, *t* and *t +1*. Equity in the amount of $2,000 is applied to this trade (calculated as $1,000 for long side shares and $1,000 for short side shares).

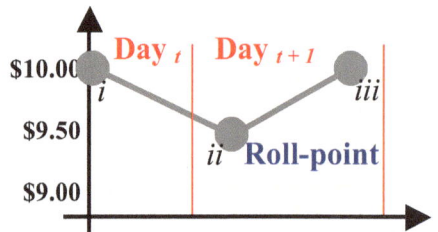

Security Price	(a) Long **Profit/** **Loss** or *Liability Coverage*	(b) Long Side Value	(c) Short Side Value	(d) Short **Profit/** **Loss** or *Liability Coverage*	(e) Stripped Cash	(f) Cash Reset as Long Side Value or Shares	Bias/ NIP**
$10.00 *i*	---	$1,000	$1,000	---	---	---	NA/0
$9.50 *ii*	-$50 3	$950	$1,050	+$50	--- 1	---	NA/0
---	$50	Maintain	Reset 2	Strip	$50.00	---	---
---	$50	$950	$950	---	$2.50	$47.50	+/5
$10.00*iii*	+$50	$1,000	$900	-$50	$2.50	$50.00	+/5
---	$100	$1,000	$900	---	$2.50	---	---

*Liability Coverage is cash held in reserve
**NIP is net investment position

The short side value amount, column (c), at the onset of the trade is cash in the amount of $1,000 from the sale of 100 borrowed security shares at $10. $1,000 is the collateral for the short shares liability. The $1,000 short side onset value amount appreciates to $1,050 as a result of a fall in the security price from $10.00 (point *i*) to $9.50 (point *ii*). The

$1,050 roll-point value amount, in **blue,** column (c), from the short side of the box trade is split and dispersed as three new amounts, starred in **red**: (1) stripped cash, (2) reset hedge, and (3) long side margin liability payment.

The first amount is $50 of stripped short side profit, identified as stripped cash in column (e), and later as whole long shares (f) and remaining stripped cash (e).

The second amount is $950, column (c), that is used as collateral to reset the box position of short shares borrowed and sold in a value equal to the current long side value, column (b).

The third and remaining amount is $50 cash, column (a), used to cover the margin liability equal to the $50 long side value loss, column (a), when the box trade is reset at the roll-point (calculated as the difference of roll-point reset value, $950, and initial collateral, $1,000).

Adding the final values from columns (a), (b), (c) and (e) totals a profit of $2.50, earned from stripped short side value exposed to the market (invested) at a security price of $9.50 on day $t+1$. No leverage is employed and the return is a modest .0125% (calculated as $2.50 divided by $2,000 (the onset sum of $1,000 long value and $1,000 short value)). This overnight, two-day trade annualizes to 25.61% per year.

Once again the following chart displays the actions and components of the prior example's hedged box trade in an alternate format.

	LONG		SHORT	ADDITION SHARES	TOTAL
$10.00 STOCK PRICE	1000	=	1000	---	2000.00
$9.50 STOCK PRICE	950		1050	---	
ROLL-POINT	950		1000	50	2000.00
HEDGE THE LONG	950	=	950 + 50 CASH	50	2000.00
$10.00 STOCK PRICE	1000		900 + 50 CASH	50 + 2.50 PROFIT	2000.00
REBALANCE	1000		1000	2.50 PROFIT	2002.50

When hedged box trades are reset at the roll-point and stripped profits are applied to the purchase of long shares, the trade components become:
  (1) stripped short profit in the form of cash equal to the value loss on the long investment (column e, row 3);
  (2) a long investment with a value loss equal to the value increase on the short position (column b, row 2);

(3) a new hedging short position share quantity value amount lower than the original by the amount of stripped short profit and equal to the current long shares investment value (column c, row 4);

(4) a cash reserve equal to the initial onset short side value minus the current short position (column a, row 3).

From the onset trade to the roll-point, the overall value movement for this investment position is zero (no gain, no loss). Instead of long security shares and short security shares alone making the whole of the investment position, cash and margin liability are now included at the roll-point. Margin liability is the amount the long side investment loses when the security share value falls. It must be repaid when a hedged box trade is closed.

Cash is the transfer of value from the security share owner to the position trader. The position trader profits from the value difference at the point when the shares are borrowed and sold to the market to the point when the position trader rebalances or closes a profitable short position. The original share owner loses value on paper because the security share price drops. That value difference now belongs to the position trader who has stripped it from that share owner, who has invested in a buy-and-hold strategy.

Consider the effect of leverage on this return. Utilizing 2:1 leverage through margin will increase the duration return from .0125% to a duration yield of .025%, annualizing to approximately 51%. Margin and trading fees are not considered.

If market sentiment is clearly bullish at point (*ii*), the short side can be closed and $1,000 or the full trade equity amount, $2,000, can be committed as an investment at a cost basis of $9.50 for a return at point (*iii*) of 5.25% (calculated [((($50 of short side profit ÷ the current price per share of $9.50 (fractional share discarded)) × $.50 share value appreciation from point *ii* to point *iii*) + $50 of short side profit) ÷ $1,000] = 5.25%).

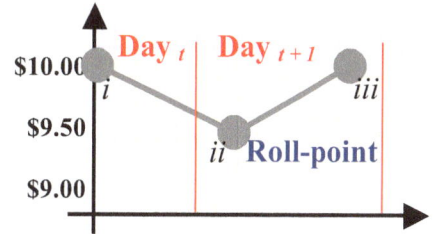

There is no profit harvesting opportunity in a perfectly hedged primary security scenario. If the security share value rises from the onset/entry point, gains can be rebalanced from the winning side of the trade (the long side) and used to cover the losses incurred by the losing side of the trade (the short side).

If one chooses not to use the profits from the long side to cover short side losses when hcdgcd box trades are reset at the rebalance point, additional collateral can be required to establish the short side of the box at the higher security price.

Rebalancing will reset the trade to its onset equilibrium, so that short side stripping opportunities can be realized immediately from a fall in share value. Choosing not to reset the trade (at the rebalance point) requires that the share value fall to its onset/entry point first before stripping opportunities arise from additional declines in share value. The long side value (after gains are rebalanced at the rebalance point) equals the initial long side value amount at the onset of the trade. The share quantity making the long side value amount is now less.

For example:

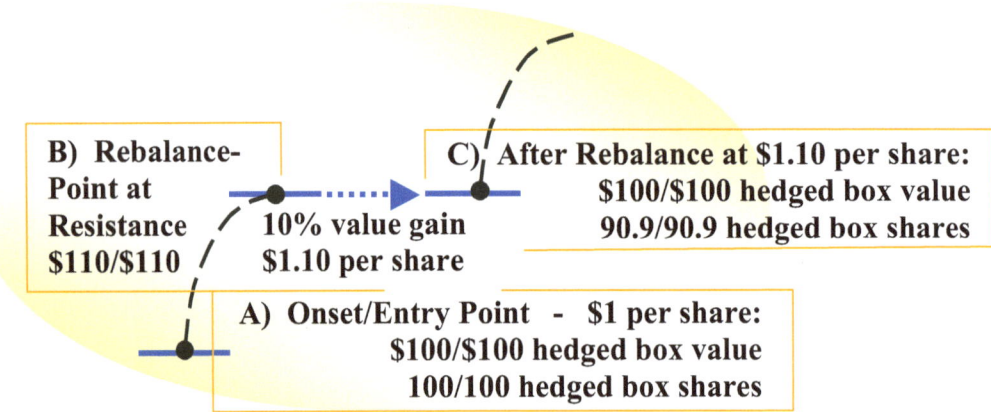

B) Rebalance-Point at Resistance $110/$110

10% value gain $1.10 per share

C) After Rebalance at $1.10 per share:
$100/$100 hedged box value
90.9/90.9 hedged box shares

A) Onset/Entry Point - $1 per share:
$100/$100 hedged box value
100/100 hedged box shares

What issues can leverage introduce into the Long/Short Hedged Box strategy? There are two issues to consider when trading a Leveraged Hedged Box Long/Short strategy. The first is the high volume of margined monies and shares that can accrue daily margin fees if the trade takes longer than expected to achieve a profit. Leverage allowed by NYSE Rule 431(e)(1) for the long/short hedged box strategy can boost share quantities into the thousands. Accordingly, the second issue working against this strategy is the potential for higher than anticipated trading fees due to higher share quantities if one's brokerage account does not provide flat rate trading. *Flat rate trading* is a fixed cost per trade regardless of share quantity.

The Mechanics Of Stripped Value Profits From Short Sales

The stripped profit value transfer works only when certain elements are in place. The investor's long investment shares from which the position trader borrows must be held in a margin account in street name, not in the investor's name. Holding shares in street name allows the investor to buy and sell shares quickly and to borrow money from the brokerage to leverage an investment. The brokerage has the responsibility to keep track of what shares are owned by which investor.

When opening a margin account, the investor gives the brokerage certain rights to the security shares deposited or transferred into the account. These shares can be lent to other traders and collateralized for money the brokerage borrows from banks. The brokerage can charge margin fees to position traders who borrow shares to sell short to the market.

Investors who use the buy-and-hold investing methodology miss opportunities to realize profits from security share value gains.

For example: An investor who owns long security shares fails to capitalize on gains when the share value appreciates to $175. The position trader, sensing a change in market sentiment from bullish to bearish, borrows the investor's shares to sell short to the market.

It is only the investor who does not profit in a falling market. The brokerage earns margin fees on the shares lent to the position trader. The position trader strips profit from the investor's shares in an amount equal to their decline in value from the point the security shares are borrowed and sold at time t_1, to the point the position trader purchases the shares from the market to close the short trade and return the borrowed shares to the brokerage at time t_2.

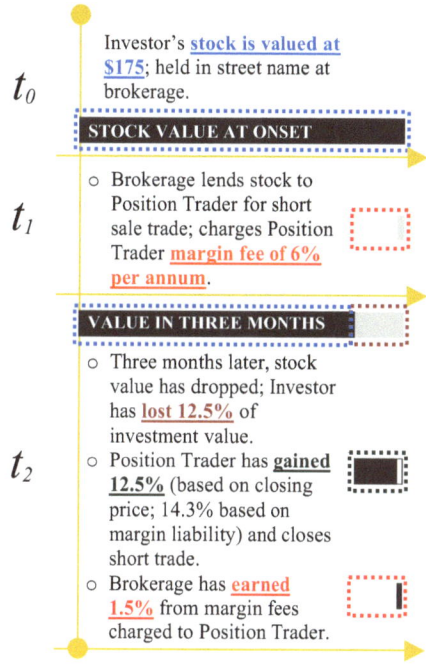

t_0 — Investor's **stock is valued at $175**; held in street name at brokerage.

STOCK VALUE AT ONSET

t_1
- Brokerage lends stock to Position Trader for short sale trade; charges Position Trader **margin fee of 6% per annum**.

VALUE IN THREE MONTHS

t_2
- Three months later, stock value has dropped; Investor has **lost 12.5%** of investment value.
- Position Trader has **gained 12.5%** (based on closing price; 14.3% based on margin liability) and closes short trade.
- Brokerage has **earned 1.5%** from margin fees charged to Position Trader.

Investors should not deposit shares into a margin account and allow the brokerage to hold those shares in street name if they do not want position traders and brokerages to profit from their investment value losses.

Conclusion

The next report in this two-part discussion of the long and short hedging methodology explains how derivative securities boost returns while reducing exposure to loss of principal risk. *The Short/Long Derivates Hedge* expands upon the instruction provided in this report by explaining how incorporating derivates into the long and short hedging methodology creates arbitrage opportunities to earn derivative income with zero possibility for principal loss.

RISK DISCLOSURE STATEMENT

It should not be assumed that concepts, models or strategies discussed, presently or in the future, will always be profitable or will equal the performance of the strategy as explained in this report.

Transactions in options carry a high degree of risk. If the option is "covered" by the seller holding a corresponding position in the underlying security or a future contract or another option, the risk may be reduced. If the option is not covered, the risk of loss can be unlimited.

Most open-outcry and electronic trading facilities are supported by computer-based component systems for the order routing, execution, matching, registration or clearing of trades. As with all facilities and systems, they are vulnerable to temporary disruption or failure. Your ability to recover certain losses may be subject to limits on liability imposed by the system provider, the market, the clearing house and/or member firms. Such limits may vary. You can ask the firm with which you deal for details in this respect.

Trading on an electronic trading system may differ not only from trading in an open-outcry market, but also from trading on other electronic trading systems. If you undertake transactions on an electronic trading system, you will be exposed to risks associated with the system including the failure of hardware and software. The result of any system failure may be that your order is either not executed according to your instructions or is not executed at all.

ACKNOWLEDGEMENT AND AGREEMENT

Receipt or use of the provided material represents acknowledgement of this disclaimer and agreement to the terms and conditions. Links provided to other websites do not imply endorsement, sponsorship, promotion or affiliation. Hedge Strategies is the copyright owner of all impersonal, indirect and general strategy educating materials and use or reproduction for any other purpose is expressly prohibited by law, and may result in civil and criminal penalties.

DISCLAIMER OF WARRANTY

The material provided by Hedge Strategies is provided "as is" with no express or implied warranty.

GENERAL DISCLAIMER

Hedge Strategies does not give personal, specific, direct or individual market advice in the strategy newsletter reports, on its website, at lectures and within other media. The purchase fee for strategy newsletter reports is non-refundable. Investments in the derivatives markets, especially ETFs, options and futures are speculative and involve substantial risk of loss of part or all applied monies. The information provided does not imply a buy, sell, or hold recommendation for one's personal positions or investments. The strategy subscriber must determine what level of risk is appropriate for his/her/its portfolio. Hedge Strategies is not a registered or licensed investment advisor, and does not provide individual, direct, personal or specific investment advice or any other legal or tax professional advice. Readers are advised to consult with an accredited broker, investment manager, registered investment advisor, or the like who understands derivative strategies before attempting to replicate any of the described strategies. All questions regarding margin or account allocation or any questions concerning your trading account are to be addressed to your broker. Consultation of a personal and professional nature with qualified licensed advisors and an independent investigation of the strategies presented in each strategy newsletter report prior to selling or buying any derivative is recommended for all Readers. All investors must read the Characteristics and Risks of Standardized Options, available on The Options Clearing Corporations' (OCC) website at http://www.theocc.com/publications/risks/riskchap1.jsp prior to trading derivatives.

LIMITATION ON LIABILITY

Liability shall be limited in the aggregate to direct and actual damages not to exceed the purchase fees received by Hedge Strategies from the Reader, whether in contract, tort, negligence, or otherwise. Hedge Strategies will not be liable for damages resulting directly, or indirectly, from the use of, or reliance upon, any material provided and is not and shall not be held liable for any loss or damages related to, either directly or indirectly, any decline in market value or loss of any position or investment and any delay or absence of material resulting from postal mailing issues and problems. Hedge Strategies is not engaged in rendering any legal, tax or professional services by placing these general, impersonal, indirect strategies on its website and therefore does not, in any way, warrant or guarantee the merchantability, fitness for a particular purpose or success of any action taken on reliance of information presented in its strategy newsletter reports or lecture statements or opinions.

RISKS

Trading derivatives is a challenging and potentially profitable opportunity for educated and experienced investors. However, before deciding to participate in derivative trading, you should carefully consider your investment objectives, level of experience and risk tolerance. Most importantly, do not invest money you cannot afford to lose. Hedge Strategies assumes no liability from losses resulting from the use of the strategy newsletter reports provided. The leveraged nature of derivative trading means that any market movement will have an equally proportional effect on deposited funds. This may work against you as well as for you. The possibility exists that you could sustain a total loss of initial margin funds and be required to deposit additional funds to maintain your investment position. If you fail to meet any margin requirement, your investment position may be liquidated and you will be responsible for any resulting losses. Derivative investment or positions within your brokerage accounts are not federally insured against losses incurred through trading. To manage exposure, employ risk-reducing strategies such as 'stop-loss' or 'contingency' orders. Any opinions, news, research, analyses, prices, or other information contained in the strategy newsletter reports, in oral lecture or on its website are provided as general market commentary, and do not constitute investment advice. Any opinions, news, research, analyses, prices, or other information contained in the strategy newsletter reports, in oral lecture or on its website are not a substitute for obtaining professional advice from a qualified person, firm or corporation. Consult the appropriate qualified professional advisor for more complete and current information.

Other Hedge Strategy Investment Reports:

 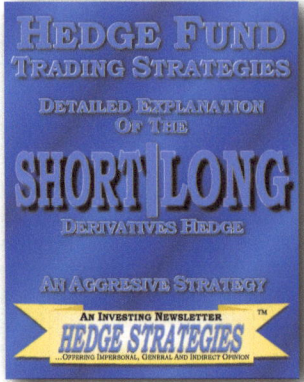 

 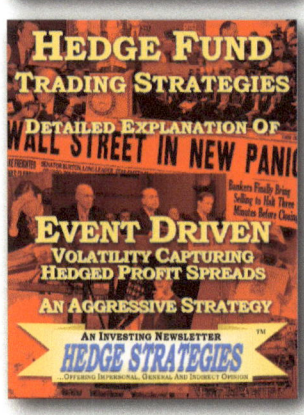 

 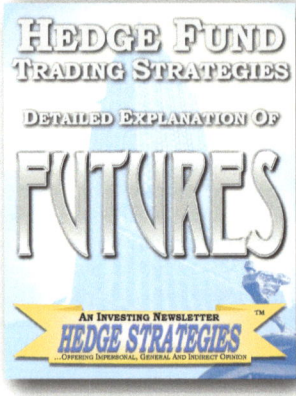